Community Workers

Keeping You Healthy

A Book About Doctors

Ann Owen
Illustrated by Eric Thomas

Thanks to our advisers for their expertise, research, knowledge, and advice:

Kelly Delahunty, M.D., St. Paul, Minnesota

Susan Kesselring, M.A., Literacy Educator
Rosemount-Apple Valley-Eagan (Minnesota) School District

PICTURE WINDOW BOOKS
Minneapolis, Minnesota

Managing Editor: Bob Temple
Creative Director: Terri Foley
Editor: Peggy Henrikson
Editorial Adviser: Andrea Cascardi
Copy Editor: Laurie Kahn
Designer: John Moldstad
Page production: Picture Window Books
The illustrations in this book were prepared digitally.

Picture Window Books
5115 Excelsior Boulevard
Suite 232
Minneapolis, MN 55416
1-877-845-8392
www.picturewindowbooks.com

Printed in the United States of America.

Library of Congress Cataloging-in-Publication Data
Owen, Ann, 1953–
Keeping you healthy : a book about doctors / written by Ann Owen ; illustrated by Eric Thomas.
p. cm. — (Community workers)
Summary: Describes some of the things that doctors do to help people stay healthy.
Includes bibliographical references and index.
ISBN 1-4048-0085-9
1. Physicians—Juvenile literature. [1. Physicians. 2. Occupations.]
I. Thomas, Eric, ill. II. Title. III. Community workers (Picture Window Books)
R690 .O95 2004
610'.92—dc21
2003004164

Many people
in your community
have jobs helping others.

What does
a doctor do?

A doctor asks you what's wrong.

My throat
is sore.

A doctor asks you how you got hurt.

I fell down playing soccer.

A doctor
shines a light
in your eyes,

takes a look
in your ears,

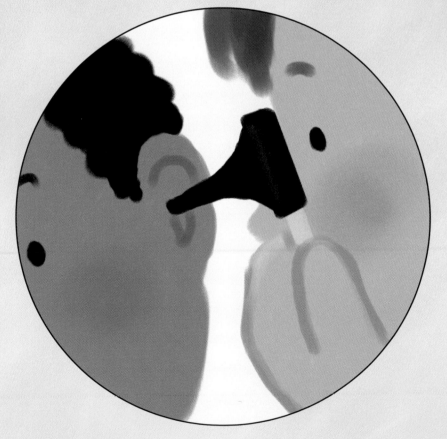

and asks you to say, "Aah."

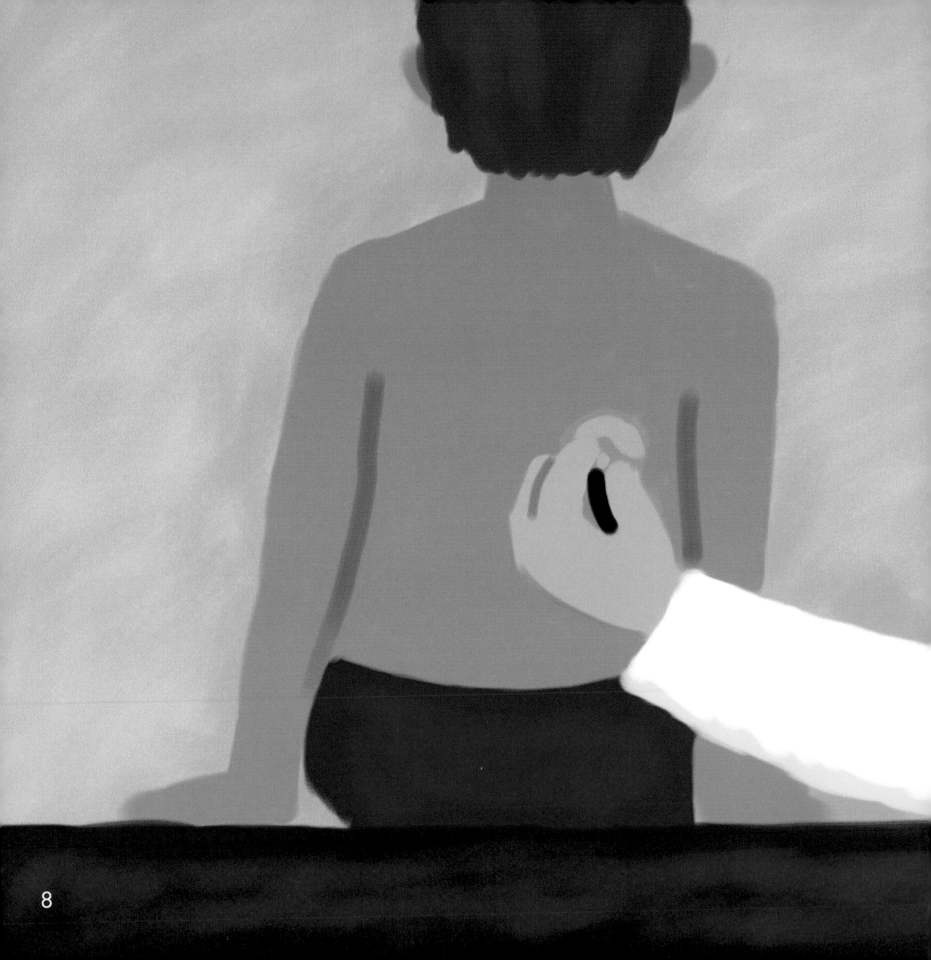

A doctor asks you to breathe deeply.

The doctor presses on your belly.

The doctor makes your leg jump.

A doctor uses tools that have big names.

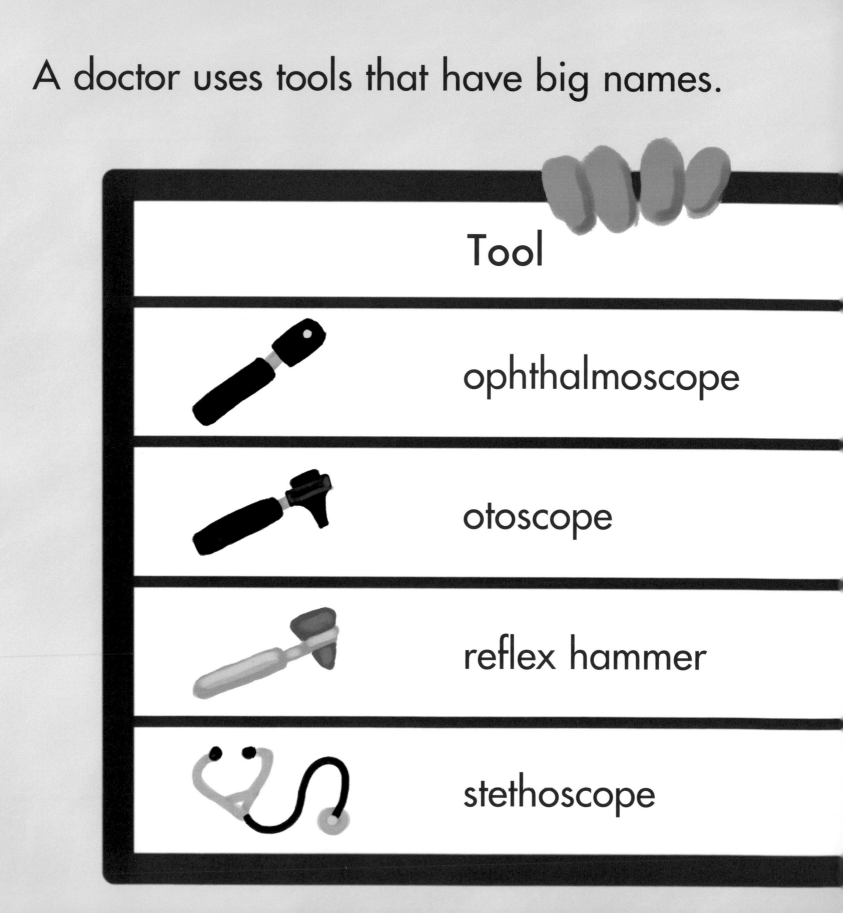

Tool	
	ophthalmoscope
	otoscope
	reflex hammer
	stethoscope

How the Doctor Uses It

to look into your eyes

to look into your ears

to tap your knee

to listen to your heart and lungs

A doctor tells you what medicine to take.

A doctor fixes you up.

What color cast would you like?

15

A doctor wears a long white coat or a loose, colorful uniform called scrubs.

Those look like pajamas.

A doctor keeps a chart about you.

You've really grown this year!

Sometimes a doctor needs to give you a shot.

This will hurt only for a few seconds.

Doctors help keep you healthy.

Did You Know?

When the doctor taps your knee with a reflex hammer, a message goes through your body to your brain. Faster than you can blink, your brain sends a message back to your leg to *jump!* By watching your leg jump, the doctor can tell if the message system in your body is working well.

Casts hold broken bones in place while they heal. At first, casts were made of white plaster. Now, doctors use casts made of a material called fiberglass. It comes in different colors. The doctor wets the fiberglass, then winds it around the broken body part and smears a gel over it. The fiberglass dries as hard as a rock. Fiberglass is much lighter and 20 times stronger than plaster.

Today, about one out of every four doctors in the United States is a woman.

Important Dates for Doctors

When	What	How Long Ago?
1660	The stethoscope was invented in France.	More than 340 years
1752	The first hospital in America opened in Philadelphia, before the United States even became a country.	About 250 years
1765	The first medical school in America opened in Philadelphia.	About 240 years
1862	Elizabeth Blackwell, the first woman doctor to be trained in the United States, graduated from medical school.	About 140 years
1880s	X-ray machines were first used.	About 120 years

Words to Know

cast (KAST) – a hard covering that keeps a broken bone in place while it heals

community (kuh-MYOO-nuh-tee) – a group of people who live in the same area

healthy (HEL-thee) – feeling good, without sickness or pain

hospital (HOSS-pi-tuhl) – a building where doctors and others work to help people who are very sick or badly hurt

medicine (MED-uh-suhn) – a substance used to help sick or injured people (or animals) get better

scrubs (SKRUHBZ) – loose, lightweight uniforms worn by some doctors in hospitals

stethoscope (STETH-uh-skope) – a tool that doctors use to listen to the heart and lungs

X-ray machine (EKS-ray muh-SHEEN) – a piece of equipment that uses very fast beams of light that you can't see to take a picture of something inside a person's body

To Learn More

At the Library

Bowman-Kruhm, Mary. *A Day in the Life of a Doctor*. New York: PowerKids Press, 1997.

Moses, Amy. *Doctors Help People*. Plymouth, Minn.: Child's World, 1997.

Ready, Dee. *Doctors*. Mankato, Minn.: Bridgestone Books, 1997.

Schaefer, Lola M. *We Need Doctors*. Mankato, Minn.: Pebble Books, 2000.

Swanson, Diane. *The Doctor and You*. Toronto: Annick Press, 2001.

On the Web

Kids Health

To learn about your body, get tips on staying healthy, or do fun activities
http://www.kidshealth.org/kid

About Children's Health

For experiments, games, and information about the human body
http://www.aboutchildrenshealth.com

Fact Hound

Want more information about doctors?
Fact Hound offers a safe, fun way to find Web sites related to this book.
All of the sites on Fact Hound have been researched by our staff.
http://www.facthound.com

1. Visit the Fact Hound home page.
2. Enter a search word related to this book, or type in this special code: 1404800859.
3. Click on the FETCH IT button.

Your trusty Fact Hound will fetch the best sites for you!